ALWAYS
BELIEVE IN THE
IMPOSSIBLE

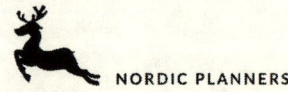 NORDIC PLANNERS

If you are enjoying this notebook, please consider leaving a review. We would appreciate it very much.

THIS NOTEBOOK BELONGS TO:

_____

YOU CAN
YOU CAN
YOU CAN

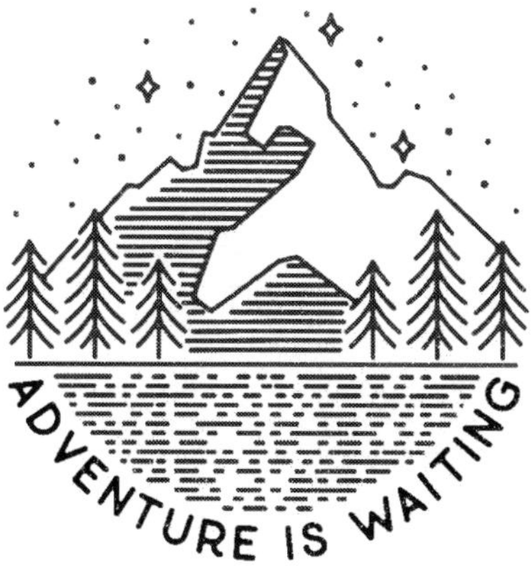
ADVENTURE IS WAITING

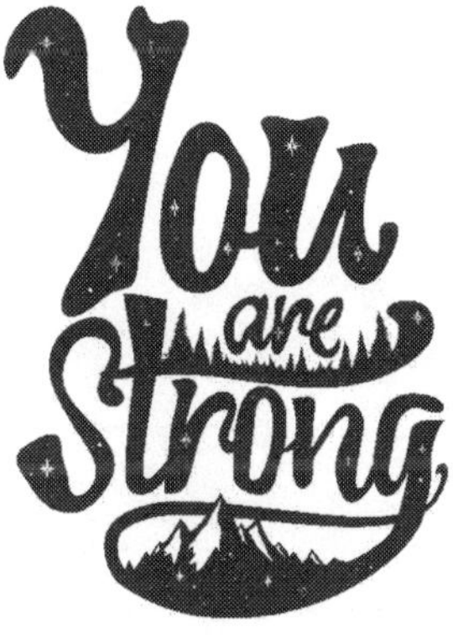
You
are
Strong

Alone, but not lonely

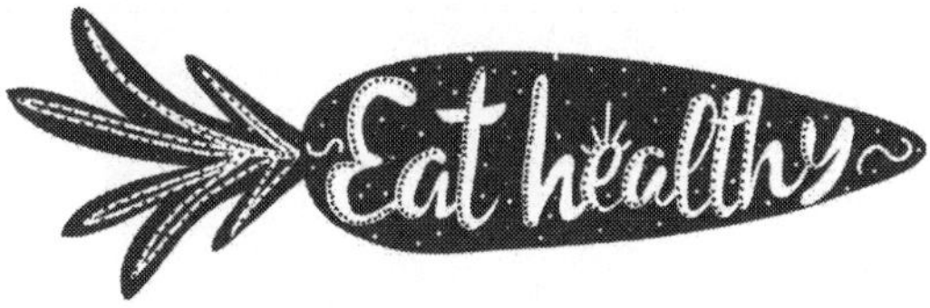
Eat healthy

always POSITVE

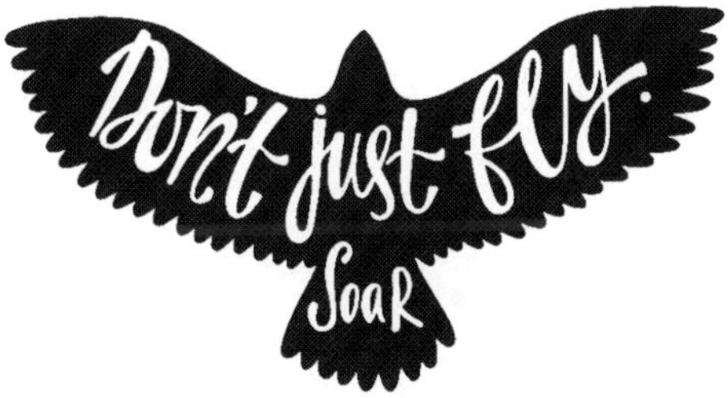
Don't just fly.
Soar

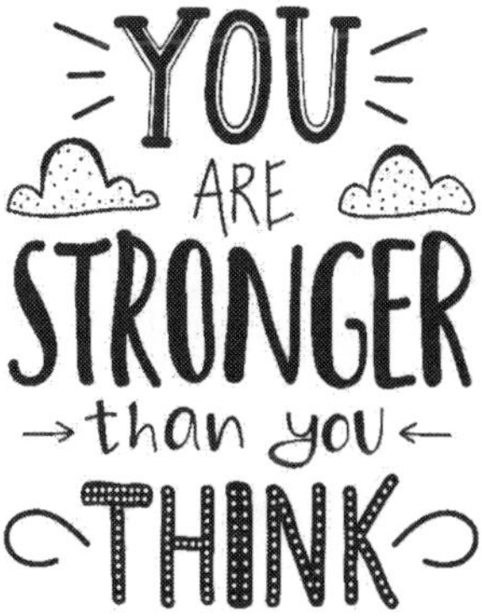
YOU
ARE
STRONGER
than you
THINK

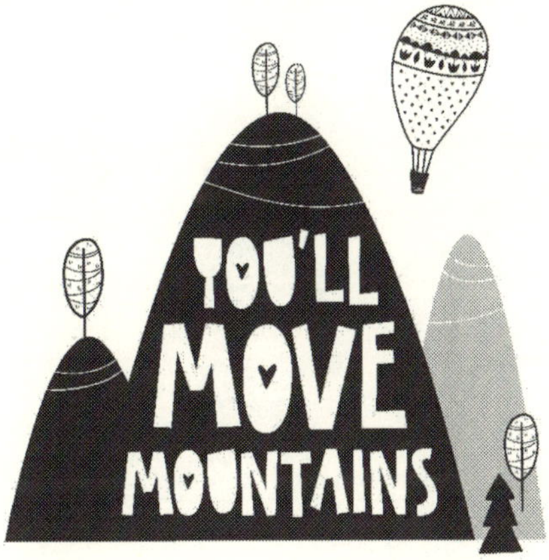
YOU'LL
MOVE
MOUNTAINS

BELIEVE IN YOURSELF

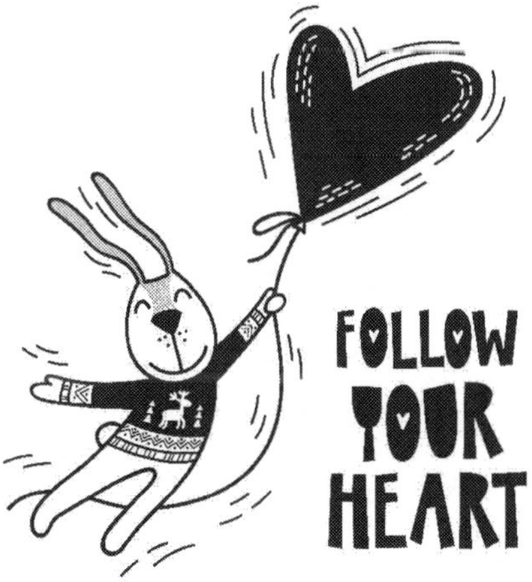
FOLLOW YOUR HEART

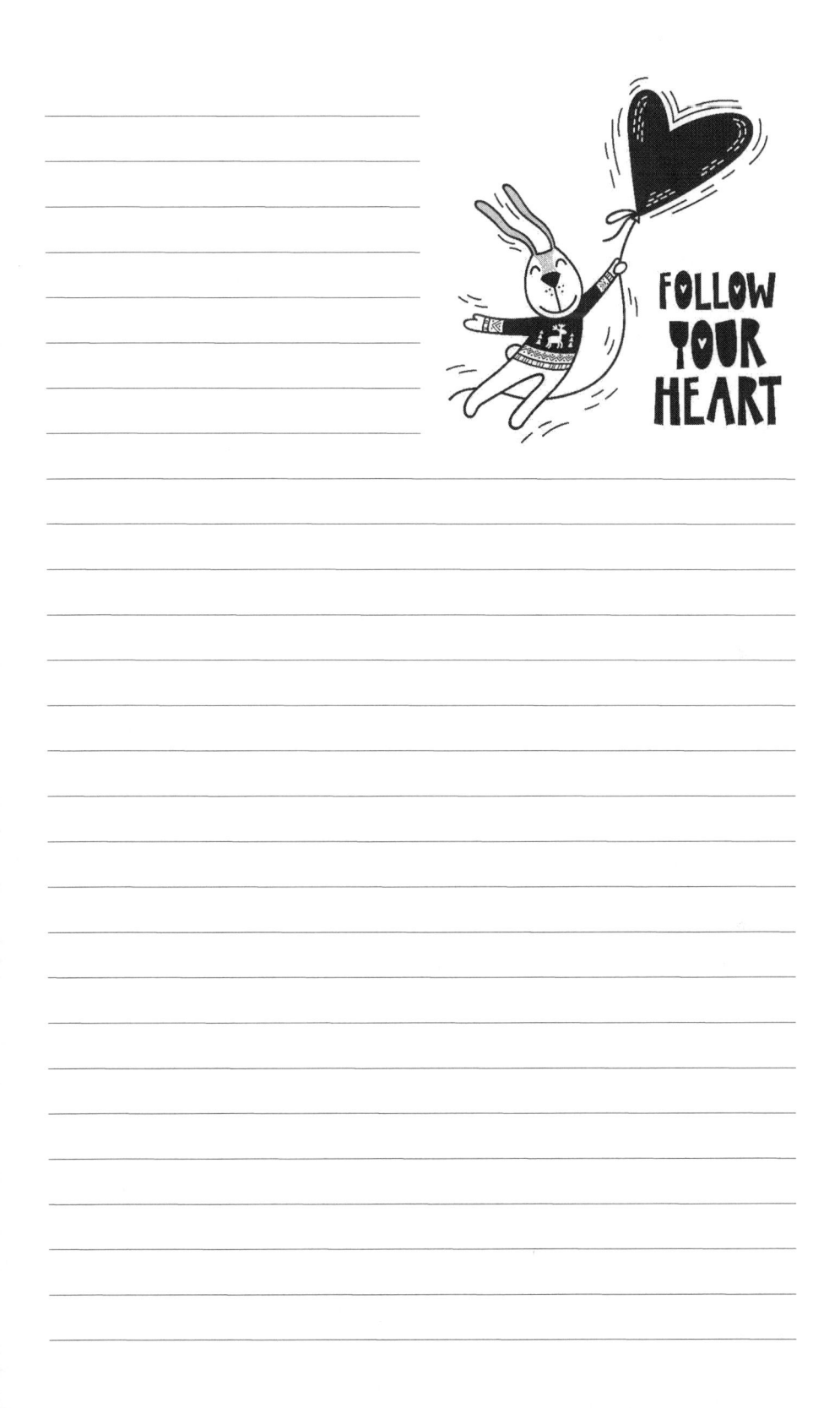

BE KIND

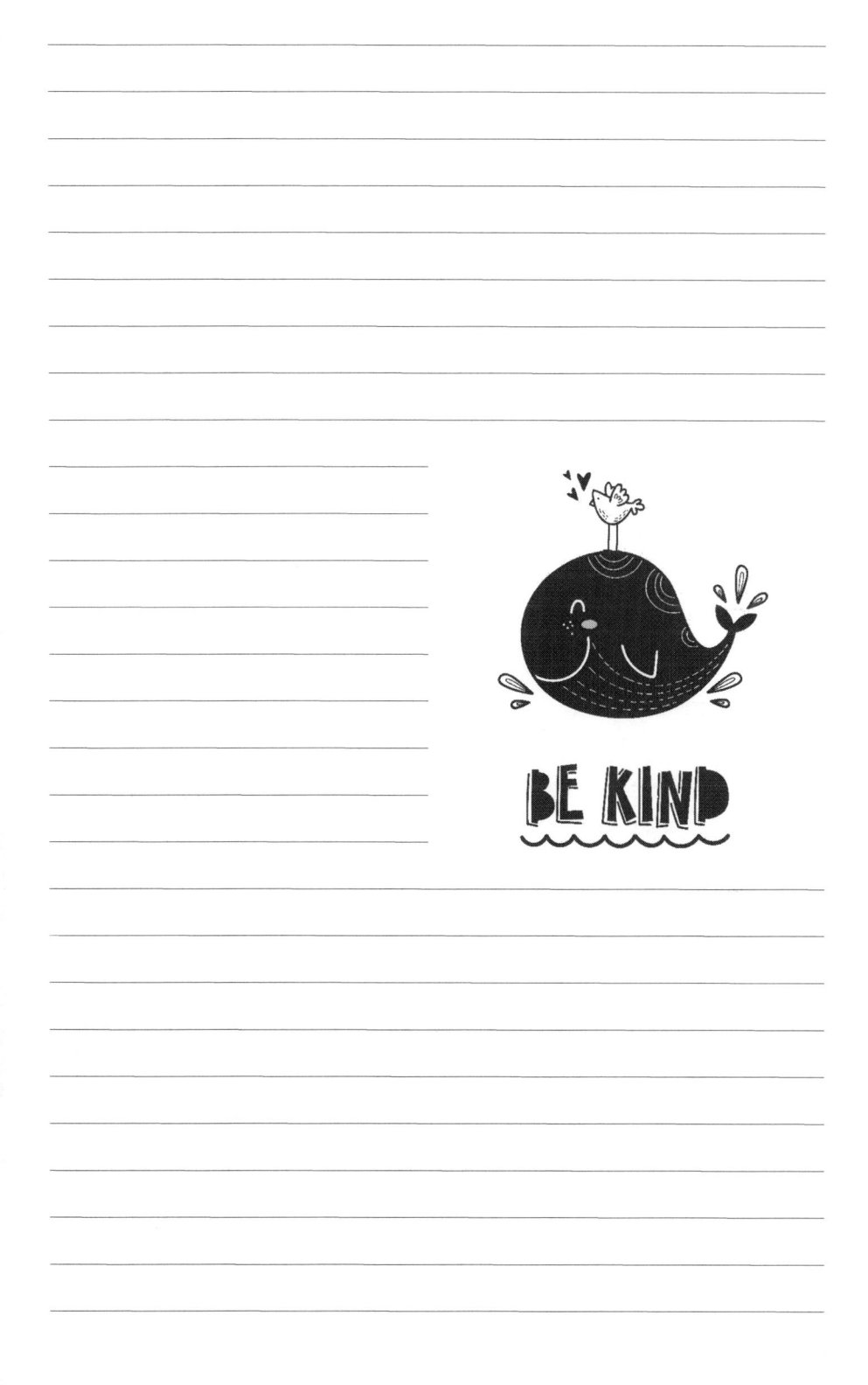

LET·YOUR HEART BE·YOUR COMPASS

HAVE
A NICE DAY

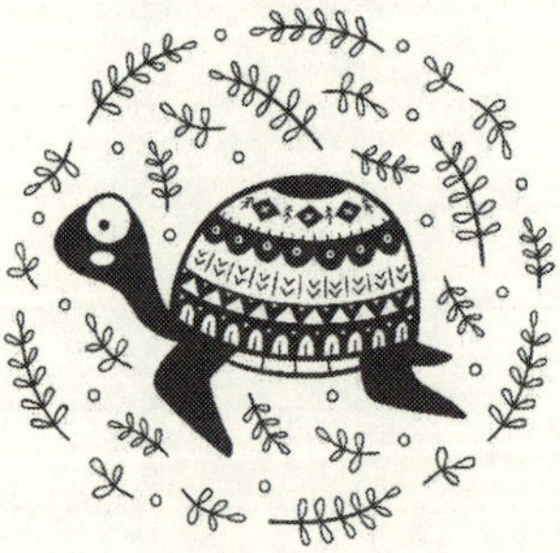

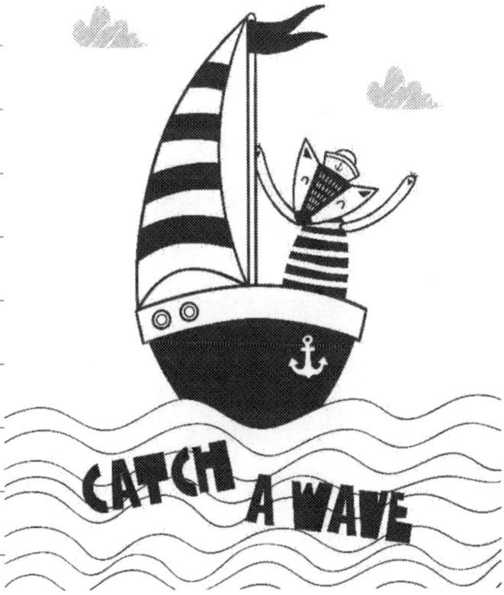
CATCH A WAVE

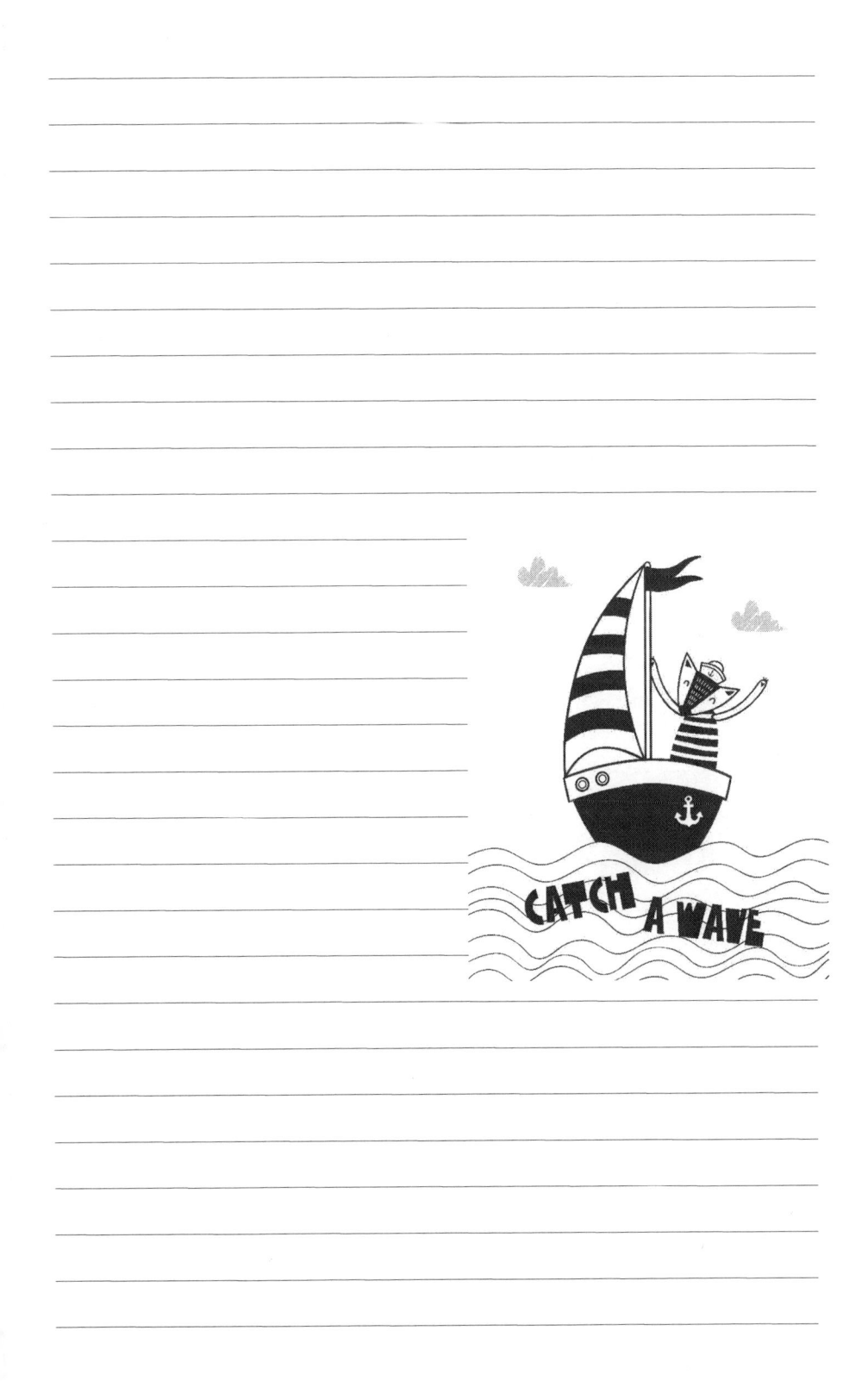

MAKE
A WISH

ENJOY LITTLE THINGS

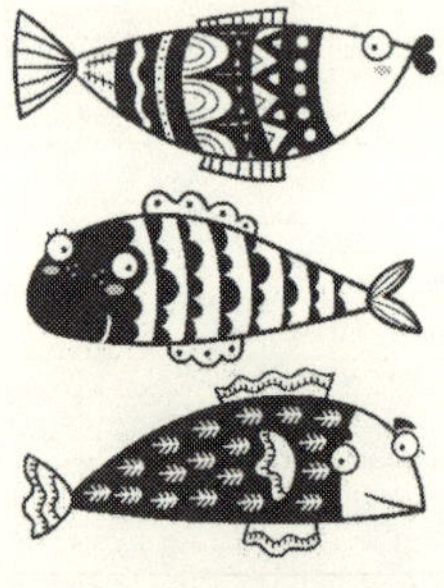

BE DIFFERENT

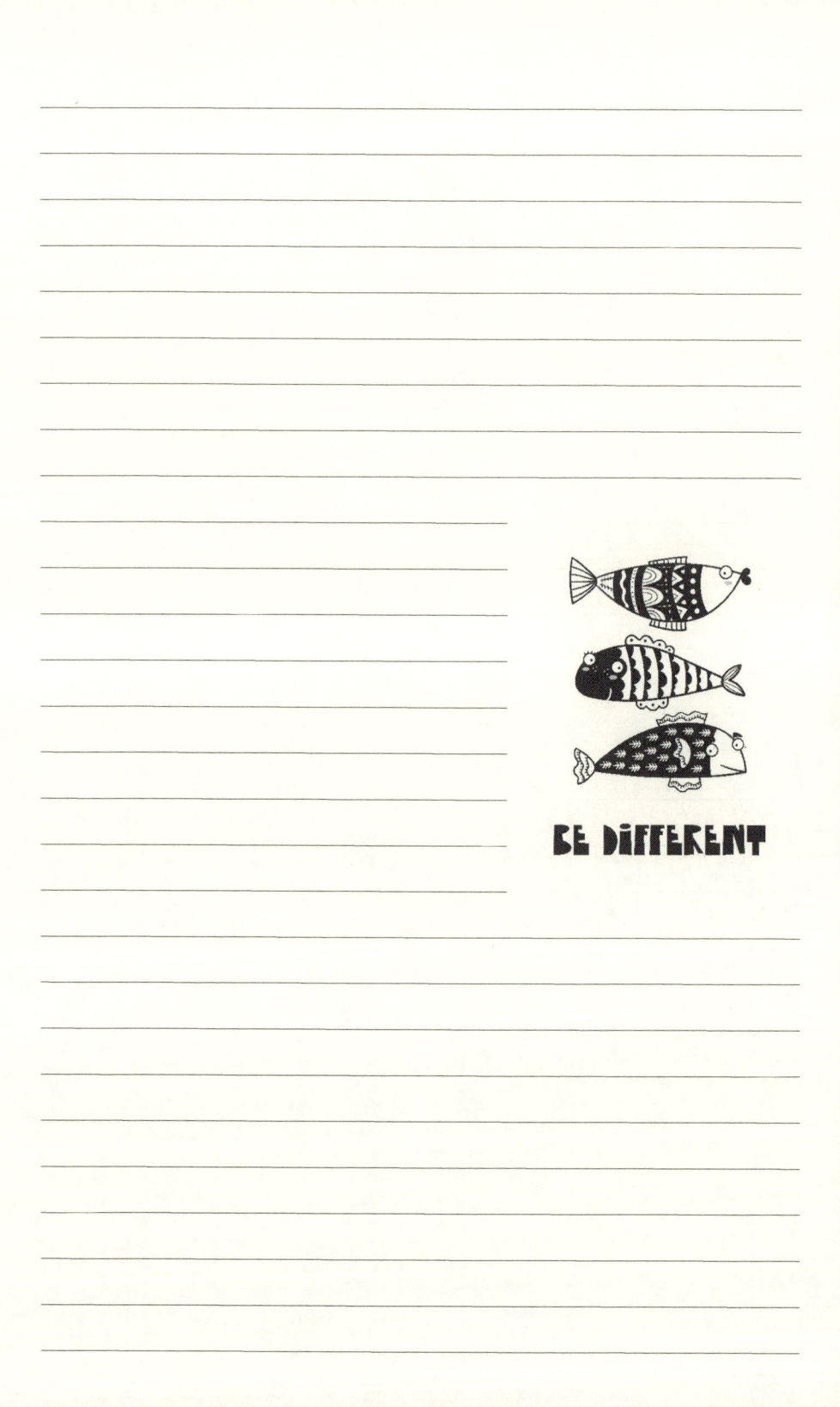

SMILE

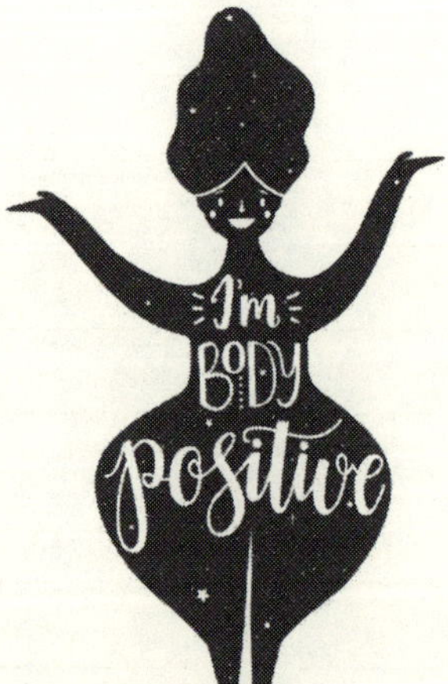
I'm
Body
positive

SUPER
HERO

YOU ARE STRONGER THAN YOU THINK

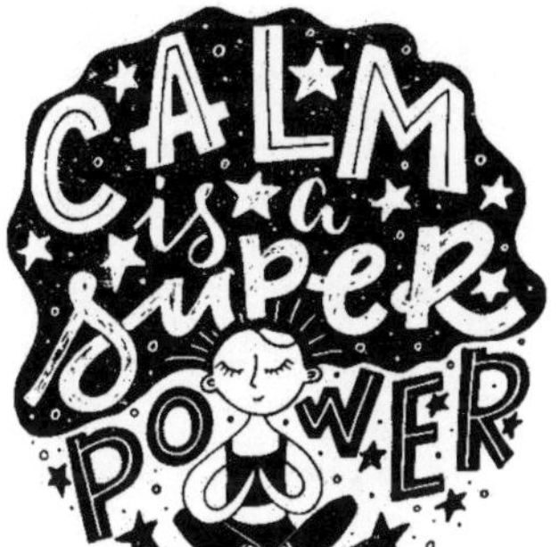
CALM
is a
super
POWER

hope

SHINE ON

LISTEN TO YOUR HEART

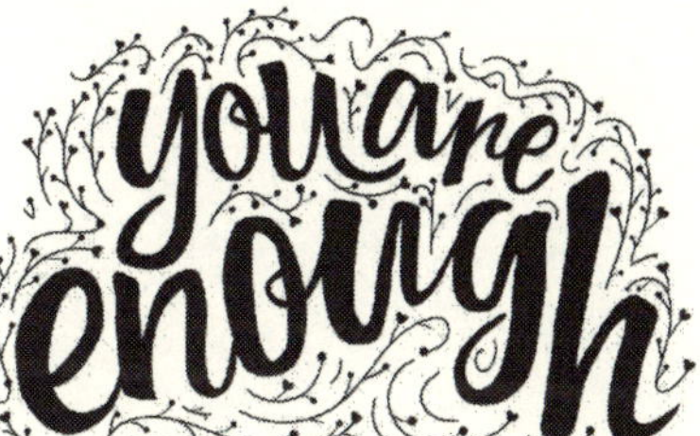
you are
enough

Made in the USA
Coppell, TX
20 December 2023